THE SCHOLARSHIP BLUEPRINT

ALEXIS LENDERMAN

JUSTIN BLACK

The mission of The Scholarship Expert is to position students to graduate debt-free while obtaining the necessary skills to maximize their college experience academically, professionally, and personally.

www.thescholarshipexpert.com

As a thank you for your purchase, We want to give you a

FREE GIFT.

Email us at
thescholarshipexpert@gmail.com.

Title the email "FREE GIFT" and we'll send you our FREE

"TEXTBOOK TIP SHEET"

or go to bit.ly/textbooktipsheet
to help you save hundreds on
textbooks!

The Scholarship Blueprint

Printed in the United States of America
Acknowledgement

Global Perspectives Publishing
3385 S. 9th St. #83
Kalamzoo, MI 49008

Dedication

You always planted the seed of higher
education by consistently saying,
"A university would be lucky to have you."
You set the standard for not only
academic excellence, but genuine love
for those around you. Without you both,
none of this would be possible. Thank
you, Aunt Bev and Uncle Giles.

Acknowledgements

Our time at Western Michigan University has been challenging but incredibly rewarding as WMU has cultivated an environment filled with leaders and trailblazers. We've learned to utilize our resources on campus while nurturing a community filled with friendship and prosperity. Resources such as Starting Gate in the Haworth College of Business were critical in helping us develop an entrepreneurial mindset. Because of WMU, Kalamazoo, Michigan will always be our home.

During our time at WMU, we had the privilege of being a part of the Seita Scholars program for foster youth in higher education. The Seita Scholars program has helped us navigate the struggles of college as foster care youth and successfully transition into our careers. The campus coaches within the Seita program has personally impacted our lives in numerous ways. Whether the Seita Scholars program was providing assistance to students over winter break or giving us step-by-step instructions on how to successfully navigate life on top of graduating, Seita has been the support system we've all needed. The Seita Scholars program will forever have a special place in our hearts.

The importance of mentorship and support is heavily underrated both academically and professionally. With the multitude of mentors we've had throughout our collegiate career, we've been able to obtain knowledge that many wouldn't have. Because of this, we've garnered years worth of wisdom and knowledge that has positioned us to grow tremendously.

Our support system in general has offered guidance that has changed the course of our lives. This would include our pastors, Kisha and Jerwan Jones, mentors Dwayne Johnson, John Mueller, John Schmitt, Will & Khadija Fobbs, Saba G., Deveta Gardner, parents Kim and Brian Switalski, among many others! We are eternally grateful for these relationships that have played a huge part in why we started The Scholarship Expert and will continue to be trailblazers.

Last, but certainly not least, thank you to all of the scholarships and fellowships that we've received to help advance our academic career and position us to prosper.

What People Are Saying About The Scholarship Expert

"Ever since I was a freshman, Alexis Lenderman has served as my biggest role model and my most valuable mentor. She pushes me to be goal-oriented and to be the best version of myself. Alexis made my semester abroad to South Africa possible. She did everything from finding me $7500 in scholarships and even booking my flights.

She did not just do the work for me though, she taught me to find resources and taught me to aim high so that I could achieve the same results on my own for all of my other future endeavors. Alexis is a woman that teaches by example. Not only is she a trailblazer for herself, she has the gift of teaching others how to blaze their own trails.
— Mikelah Snell

"My students found Alexis to be a true inspiration! After sharing her engaging story of surviving the foster care system and her tips on finding scholarship money, several of my students were successful in getting scholarships for themselves. Alexis showed my students the importance of perseverance and why they should never give up! Alexis truly is "The Scholarship Expert."
— Mr. Kowal, Educator

"Alexis offers great advice when it comes to scholarships, job hunting, networking, and overall life advice. She has been instrumental in my learning how to apply for incredible opportunities. It was her influence that inspired me to apply and accept an internship in Washington D.C. for the summer. Alexis is savvy, intelligent, and a great mentor to me. I recommend her well-rounded expertise. A true boss lady!"
— Morgan Murray

"Alexis has a unique ability to connect with students and help them navigate the world of financial aid. Her advice and guidance is second to none. My students were engaged and determined to build a repertoire of application resources so they too, can take advantage of the millions of dollars of financial aid available. Her knowledge and tenacity is second to none. I fully endorse Alexis in all her endeavors."
— Mrs. Malsbury, Educator

"Alexis has has guided me in the direction of opportunities that I would never have dreamed of being able to be a part of without her in my corner. She has helped me acquire over $5,000+ in scholarships and admissions into programs that have helped me mature professionally."
— Chehab Kaakarli

Introduction

Combined, we graduated with over $340,000 in scholarship funding. Seeing the success we have obtained would be irresponsible f we withhold the resources we've developed. Through trial and error, we've formulated methods of discovering scholarships that have been successful throughout our collegiate career. These techniques have taken us years to perfect.

In The Scholarship Blueprint book, we've organized the exact step-by-step strategies that we've used to help you master the techniques of finding and applying for scholarship in a matter of hours.

Along with our noticeable success, we've been denied for dozens of scholarships, internships, and opportunities overall. These strategies we've used are not intended to be guaranteed, but moreover improve your chances of success within every opportunity you apply for.

There's success in numbers! The more you apply for, the higher your chances are to receive funding!

This is a guide but the work is up to YOU.

Techniques of graduating debt-free and receiving scholarship funding are almost nearly non-exist.

With the methods used in this book, we can assure you that you'll have the tools to become your own scholarship expert.

TABLE OF CONTENTS

STEPS TO APPLYING FOR SCHOLARSHIPS

1. Timeline
2. Know the institution you plan to apply for and its type
3. Calculate need
4. Brainstorm keywords: Use the Areas of Possible Scholarships worksheet
5. Start with Google by using keywords from the Areas of Possible Scholarships Worksheet
6. Use the Scholarship Tracking Worksheet to keep track of all the scholarships you're finding
7. Writing scholarship essays and personal statements
8. Letters of recommendation
9. Compile and verify
10. Submit!

*These are the EXACT steps that we've used

MINDSET OF SCHOLARSHIP WINNERS

Keys to winning scholarships:

Time and mindset
- Learn to be uncomfortable - you'll never grow where you're comfortable.
- You are your brand. What you say and do matters! Think about your legacy and what you want to leave behind.
- Relationships matter! Utilize your network and those around you.
- Develop (or continue developing) habits of service - giving back to your community.
- Always be prepared to learn and take notes.

According to researcher Carol Dweck, there are two types of mindsets: A fixed mindset and a growth mindset.

In a fixed mindset, people believe their qualities are fixed traits and therefore cannot change. They believe that talent alone leads to success, and effort is not required.

Alternatively, in a growth mindset, people believe that their learning and intelligence can grow with time and experience.

The main difference between the two mindsets is the belief in the permanence of intelligence and ability; one views it as very permanent, with little to no room for change in either direction, why the other views it as more changeable, with opportunities for improvement.

When people believe they can become smarter, they realize that their effort has an effect on their success, so they put in extra time, leading to higher achievement.

With a growth mindset, individuals may achieve more than others because they are worrying less about looking intelligent and putting more of their energy into learning.

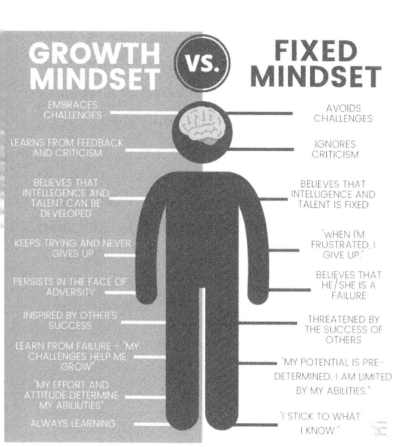

GROWTH MINDSET **VS.** FIXED MINDSET

Growth Mindset:
- EMBRACES CHALLENGES
- LEARNS FROM FEEDBACK AND CRITICISM
- BELIEVES THAT INTELLEGENCE AND TALENT CAN BE DEVELOPED
- KEEPS TRYING AND NEVER GIVES UP
- PERSISTS IN THE FACE OF ADVERSITY
- INSPIRED BY OTHER'S SUCCESS
- LEARN FROM FAILURE - "MY CHALLENGES HELP ME GROW"
- "MY EFFORT AND ATTITUDE DETERMINE MY ABILIUTIES"
- ALWAYS LEARNING

Fixed Mindset:
- AVOIDS CHALLENGES
- IGNORES CRITICISM
- BELIEVES THAT INTELLIGENCE AND TALENT IS FIXED
- "WHEN I'M FRUSTRATED, I GIVE UP."
- BELIEVES THAT HE/SHE IS A FAILURE
- THREATENED BY THE SUCCESS OF OTHERS
- "MY POTENTIAL IS PRE-DETERMINED. I AM LIMITED BY MY ABILITIES."
- "I STICK TO WHAT I KNOW."

TIMELINE

Primetime Scholarship Season is from August-December, but there's a focus on October and March. Awards are typically for the following school year.

Most scholarship awards are oriented to students starting in the fall, that doesn't mean that those who decide to begin their college journey in the spring or summer are out of luck!

EARLY/PRIORITY ADMISSIONS VS. REGULAR ADMISSIONS

If you're a high school senior, I would recommend taking advantage of the early/priority admission period. Schools admit the majority of students during the early admissions period which gives students an advantage when applying. Many deadlines are November 1st or November 15th. Some are as early as October 15th.

FAFSA opens in October. This is first-come-first serve federal aid, so you need to submit your application as soon as possible.

WHY YOU SHOULD APPLY EARLY:

- SEVERAL STATES HAVE FIRST-COME, FIRST-SERVED FINANCIAL AID PROGRAMS
- TO MEET STATE AND SCHOOL DEADLINES

EXPERT TIP:

Keep searching for scholarships throughout the year. Some scholarships may provide funds at different points in the year, especially if they select new winners for each semester.

TYPES OF INSTITUTIONS

PUBLIC VS. PRIVATE

Public	Private
- Primarily funded by a state government - Generally larger than private schools and have larger class sizes	- Operates as an educational nonprofit organization that does not receive its primary funding from a state government - Generally smaller and have smaller class sizes than public schools - Some may have religious affiliations

MYTH: Well-known and private schools always cost more.

Actually, schools such as Princeton, Cornell, University of Michigan, and several others offer full-tuition and room & board scholarships for low-income students. In fact, the average net price of tuition and fees in 2019 was $14,610 at private nonprofit four-year schools. These students typically receive an average of $21,220 in grant aid and tax benefits (CNBC, 2019). So when you factor in scholarships and grants, the schools could be very affordable to attend.

Community Colleges typically offer two years degrees and/or general education courses that often-time transfer to a four-year institution. Costs can be as little as $3,500 a year to attend. For pell grant recipients, the cost could be fully covered. Depending on your city or state, a community college near you may be covered by a College Promise program.

EXPERT TIPS:

- Contact both the community college and university you plan to attend to ensure your credits will transfer.
- Some community colleges provide more support for non-traditional students such as student-parents, adult students, etc.

Trade Schools are designed to provide vocational or technical skills (e.g. welding and cosmetology).

WHAT IS FINANCIAL AID?

Money to help pay for college or trade school such as work-study, loans, and scholarships. Oftentimes these are based upon your household income.

FAFSA: The Free Application for Federal Student Aid is a form completed by current and prospective college students in the United States to determine their eligibility for student financial aid.

Only 45% of high school students completed and filed the FAFSA in the 2018-19 school year.

This means that less than half of graduating high school students are applying for federal financial aid. Students who don't complete FAFSA are missing out on their share of billions in financial aid (CNBC, 2019) - DON'T LET THIS BE YOU!

FAFSA funds are distributed on a first-come, first-serve basis.

Pell Grant: Federal Pell Grants are usually awarded only to undergraduate students who display exceptional financial need and have not earned a bachelor's, graduate, or professional degree. If you are pell grant eligible you could receive up to $6,197. This is also on a first come first serve basis!

MYTHS:

- There is an income cut-off to apply for federal student aid. - Being "too rich" only applies to less than 5% of the U.S. population.
- Missing the deadline - even if you applied for FASFA after October, still complete the FAFSA for an opportunity to receive funding!

EVERYONE who plans on going to college should apply for FAFSA.

2019 STUDENT LOAN SNAPSHOT

MYTH: YOU NEED LOANS TO GRADUATE

Average Student Loan Debt Statistics:

- $1.61 trillion: the total amount of outstanding student loan debt
- $28,565: the average student loan debt per borrower from the Class of 2018
- $16,649: the average student loan debt per graduate from the Class of 2018
- 57%: the percentage of graduates from the Class of 2018 with student debt
- 10.9%: the percentage of student debt that is 90+ days delinquent or in default
- $393: the average monthly student loan payment for borrowers with loans not in delinquency or default

LOANS

Types of Loans		Average Interest Rate
Private Loans	Offered by a private-sector lender	7.99%, usually variable (2019)
Federal Loans	Offered by the government (generally lower interest rate).	4.45% for undergrad, fixed; 6% for graduates, fixed (2019)
Subsidized Loans	Federal loans that do not accrue interest while you are in school at least half-time or during deferment periods. Payments begin 6 months after graduation. Must demonstrate financial need.	The Education Department pays interest until 6 months post graduation
Unsubsidized Loans	Federal loans that begin to accrue interest immediately after it is disbursed. Don't need to demonstrate financial need.	Interest starts accumulating immediately with a higher interest rate than subsidized

Federal and Direct Subsidized Loans have slightly better terms to help out students with financial need (Studentaid.ed.gov).

If you decide to take out loans, make sure you KNOW and keep track of the following:

- Interest rates
- Term of repayment
- Exactly how much debt you have with a repayment plan

If you already have loans:

Look at The National Student Loan Data (NSLDS) for the exact amount of loans you have and to find your loan servicer.

SCHOLARSHIPS

MONEY YOU DON'T HAVE TO PAY BACK

Type of Scholarships	Description
Local	Typically only for students of a certain high school, district, or county. Pay attention to deadlines as they tend to have abnormal deadlines (January and June).
Institutional	Scholarship awards given by higher education institutions.
Regional	For a specific geographic region.
National	Open to students across the United States.

High School Tips:

Utilize your guidance counselors. A lot of local scholarships are paper applications and need to be mailed; ask where those applications are. Look at other high schools in your district to see what's offered to their students.

MERIT VS. NEED BASED SCHOLARSHIPS

Merit:

The scholarships are based on a student's academic or subject-specific achievement. Another example of a merit based scholarship is for a student's athleticism or talent such as music or art. Other parameters include applicants' intended majors, levels of community service, residencies in a particular state, students of color, and other qualifications.

Always be on a pursuit of excellence by being better than you were yesterday!

Need:

These scholarships take into account your current college budget into account. This includes your Expected Family Contribution (EFC), which is determined by your FAFSA.

Three Categories of University Scholarships

1. * **University**: Scholarships available to all students registered at the university
2. * **College**: A smaller institution that typically offers undergraduate degrees (i.e. College of Arts and Science or a Business College at a university)
3. * **Academic Department**: A division of a university or school faculty devoted to a particular academic discipline. Most scholarships in the department are decided by deans and faculty

AN EXAMPLE:

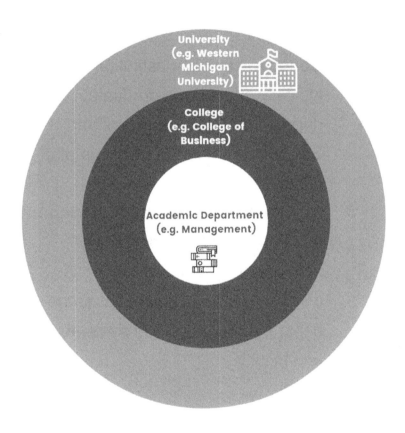

University
(e.g. Western
Michigan
University)

College
(e.g. College of
Business)

Academic Department
(e.g. Management)

OTHER TYPES OF SCHOLARSHIPS

Endowment scholarships:
A major gift to a college or university used to fund scholarships, typically in honor of a donor's loved one or the donor him/herself. Universities typically have a separate endowment scholarship application.

Athletic scholarships:
Scholarship based dominantly on his or her ability to play in a sport. Athletic scholarships are common in the United States, but in many countries they are rare or non-existent. These type of scholarship may conflict with the variety of degrees you are eligible for.

OTHER FORMS OF AID

Grants:

Often called "gift aid" because they are free money Dash financially that does not have to be repaid. Grants can come from the federal government, state government, college, or nonprofit organization.

Work-study:

Federal work-study provides part-time jobs for undergraduate and graduate students with financial need, allowing them to earn money to pay help pay education expenses. Be sure to accept it if offered - if you do not accept it when initially offered, you may not be eligible in the future.

Resident Assistant:

The resident assistant position often offers full room and board. Some universities may offer a payment to resident assistants. This can easily cover half of your college expenses, leaving you to only cover books and tuition.

HOW TO FIND SCHOLARSHIPS

CALCULATING NEED

Take into account your budget, including tuition, room and board and other college/ university expenses.

THE PROCESS

1. Brainstorm keywords: Use the Areas of Possible Scholarships (available at thescholarshipexpert.com)

2. Start with Google!

3. Use the Scholarship Tracking Worksheet (available at thescholarshipexpert.com) to keep track of all the scholarships you're finding!

BONUS:
SCHOLARSHIP DATABASES

Scholarship databases are websites and apps that can host thousands of scholarships. Here are a few databases to help you get started:

- Unigo

- Scholly (also an app)

- Fastweb.com

- Scholarships360

- Scholarships.com

- Cappex

- Chegg Scholarships

SCHOLARSHIP REQUIREMENTS

Create your own checklist of what's required in the application.

EXAMPLE:

SCHOLARSHIP APPLICATION CHECKLIST

- [ ] SCHOLARSHIP APPLICATION
- [ ] ESSAY(S)
- [ ] TRANSCRIPT/GRADES
- [ ] COMMUNITY SERVICE HOURS
- [ ] LETTER(S) OF RECOMMENDATION
- [ ] COMPLETED FAFSA
- [ ] DATE SUBMITTED: _____

30 SECOND COMMERCIAL

Before you write your essays, I recommend that you come up with a 30 second commercial that will give you additional talking points. This can also be useful when writing resumes/cover letters, writing emails to employers, or when leaving voicemails.

Your 30-second commercial should:

- Identify who you are

- Highlight a few strengths and accomplishments

- Show how you can bring added value to an organization/ business/college

- Be concise and confident

Example Script:

- Greeting: Hello, my name is

    _____.

- Experience: I am a _____
    studying _____ at

    _____.

- Interest/Passion: I am mainly
    interested in

    _____.

- Strengths: My strengths include
    _____, _____ and

    _____.

- Brief Example: Last summer, I
    worked at _____ and was
    able to _____.
- Goal: I am looking to gain further
    experience in _____.

ESSAYS

What are donors looking for in an essay?
Someone who is:

- A forward thinker
- An innovator
- A community leader
- A role model

If you're applying for college, the admissions office wants to know why this college. Always try to relate back to the mission of the college/organization/ scholarship.

NOTE: This may be uncomfortable - but you have to feel comfortable with discussing your accomplishments.

Create at least a two page or 500 word essay for each of the following:

- Your life goals and where you see yourself in five years. Be as detailed as possible.
- Some of the toughest challenges you've had to overcome.
- The colleges you are interested in and the programs you plan to apply for within the university. Why this program? What would you bring to this program and what would the program do for you?
- More essay prompts are available at thecommonapp.org.

Once your scholarship essays are written, ask a few friends, teachers, relatives, mentors or coaches to read over your essay. We would also recommend visiting the writing center.

Scholarships are giving you money to go to college and invest in your future, so how you present/carry yourself matters - as someone **worthy** of being invested in.

This is especially important on social media. Social media posts regarding drugs and alcohol will not reflect well on your character.

Essay Tips:

- For local scholarships: discuss the impact you've had in your community. Analyze a specific issue and strategize ways you plan to improve the community.
- For departmental scholarships: think about how the decision to choose your career path has impacted you? How has the skills learned from your degree translating into your career?
- Have a master essay that answers a combination of the essay prompts - then tailor this for most other essays. This process will get much easier with each application you do!

EXPERT TIPS:

- Use the Thesaurus for synonyms
- Use Transition words (e.g. therefore, meanwhile, etc.) to help your essay flow.
- Be clear and concise

PERSONAL STATEMENTS

Whether you're applying for college or for a scholarship, committee members or advisors are looking at you as a whole person rather than just your GPA. This is a good thing! You want to use your personal statement to leave an impact on the reader.

If you'd like the complete step-by-step walk through on how to perfect your personal statement, then you should check out The Scholarship Blueprint course at here.

Your story is worth being told!

LETTERS OF RECOMMENDATION

- Create a list of people who can speak about your academic and professional progression in a credible and detailed manner (teacher/professors, mentors, coaches, community members) for your letter of recommendation - NO family or friends
- Keep track of your community service
- Be strategic: ask someone that's possibly connected to the organization OR related to the field
  - Ask someone who is familiar with the subject of the scholarship

EXPERT TIPS:

- Avoid asking for a letter of recommendation from people you have a personal relationship with (family and friends)
- We highly recommend sending your resume to the person you are asking to write you a letter

COMMON MISTAKES

Missing components of the application: Follow the directions specifically as they are given. If you miss any component of the application, your application will be voided.

Procrastination: Students often wait until last minute to ask for their letter(s) of recommendation or to complete their scholarship essays. Both require weeks to prepare for!

Grammatical errors within your essay: Proofreading your essays before submission is critical. Ask someone from your network for help when reading over scholarship essays. If possible, visit a writing center.

COMPILE AND SUBMIT

Once you feel confident with your essays and all other pieces of your application, then it's time to submit!

"Success is not about your resources. It's about how resourceful you are with what you have!"
- Tony Robbins

The Scholarship Blueprint

ONLINE COURSE

Includes:

- One-hour course taught by the founder
- The Scholarship Blueprint ebook
- 8 bonus documents

WE'VE EARNED OVER

$370,000

IN SCHOLARSHIPS AND WOULD LIKE TO TEACH YOU ALL THAT WE'VE LEARNED.

Become your OWN scholarship expert!

 Available at www.thescholarshipexpert.com

*Payment plants available
*For U.S. and international students wishing to study in the U.S.

THE PERFECT COLLEGE STUDENT PLANNER

Designed By Students For Students

SIMPLE
Simple to use. Includes tip sheets to help you plan, stay organized and be efficient.

ORGANIZED
Each day is broken down by the half-hour to help you maximize your day. This includes a daily priority/to-do list.

IMPACTFUL
Daily motivational quotes to keep you going when the semester gets difficult!

 Available at perfectcollegestudentplanner.com

What Students Are Saying About The Perfect College Student Planner:

"Having this resource available to me has allowed me to create more structure in my life and become more responsible. I've learned how to increase my time management skills and be more intentional about how I use my time."
– Ashley, student

"Once I put those [tips] into practice, I saw my productivity increase tenfold. I started to use my time more wisely and get more done with less procrastination. This semester has been my most successful in the classroom and out of the classroom."
– Ellis, student

MEET THE TEAM

Alexis Lenderman is a recent graduate of Western Michigan University with two degrees, a BBA and BA in Entrepreneurship and Global & International Studies with a certificate in Nonprofit Leadership a minor in Political Science. During undergrad, she studied abroad eight times visiting South Africa, India, the Dominican Republic, South Korea, Italy, Ecuador, Senegal, and Hong Kong. All of these programs were covered by scholarships or grants.

She graduated with over $200,000 in scholarships!

From years of trial and error, she's developed techniques to help students be successful in their college career starting from before they decide on which college to attend until after they've graduated. In 2016, she founded The Scholarship Expert to help students graduate debt-free. Alexis is on a mission to help students feel empowered, yet informed to make decisions that will impact their future.

Justin Black is graduating from Western Michigan University with a degree in Public Relations and African Studies with a certificate in Nonprofit Leadership. He studied abroad five times, visiting: South Africa, Senegal, the Dominican Republic, South Korea, and Hong Kong covering a variety of topics such as community sustainability and political economics. All of these programs have been covered by scholarships or grants. Such as the Benjamin Gilman International Scholarship.

In June 2020, he is graduating debt-free with over $170,000 in scholarships!

He is determined to position black and brown students to receive funding and opportunities to further benefit the future of their community. The goal is to help more students graduate college with limited debt as they transition into their career. Justin believes success is a community effort and navigating students through higher education is a must. To do so, we must fix our minds on our future and how to help our fellow students.

Both Alexis and Justin have received a CGI U Commitment-Maker seal for their work in their communities.

A CGI U Commitment-Maker is a student who has demonstrated a clear passion for change and has developed a Commitment to Action that is new, specific, and measurable in one of CGI U's five focus areas: Education, Environment and Climate Change, Peace and Human Rights, Poverty Alleviation, or Public Health. Commitment-Makers are part of a growing community of leaders on college campuses around the world who are turning their ideas into action.

Stay Connected:

@TheScholarshipExpert
@ScholarshipXprt

Made in the USA
Las Vegas, NV
25 November 2024

12653834R00036